SOLAR MATTER
MATÉRIA SOLAR

Eugénio de Andrade

Translated by Alexis Levitin

QED Press
Fort Bragg, California

Solar Matter / Matéria Solar by Eugénio de Andrade
Translated by Alexis Levitin

QED Press
155 Cypress Street
Fort Bragg, CA 95437
(707) 964-9520 Fax: (707) 964-7531

Cataloging-in-Publications Data
Andrade, Eugénio de.
  [Matéria solar. English and Portuguese]
  Solar matter = Matéria Solar / Eugénio de Andrade :
translated by Alexis Levitin
    p. cm.
  ISBN 0-936609-34-6
  1. Andrade, Eugénio de.— Translations into English.
I. Levitin, Alexis. II. Title. III. Title: Matéria Solar.
PQ9261.A67S6513 1994
869.1'42—dc20   94-26801
                                                                CIP
Cover design and illustration by Mark Gatter

Publication of this book was supported by a Translation Grant
from The National Library and Book Institute of
Lisbon, Portugal *(Instituto da Biblioteca Nacional e do
Livro, Lisboa),* and with the assistance of the Camões
Institute of Lisbon *(Instituto Camões).*

Manufactured in the U.S.A.
First edition

Acknowledgments

Many of the translations in this volume have already appeared in the following literary magazines, whose editors we would like to thank for permission to reprint:

Cafe Solo	Christopher Street
Confrontation	Cutbank
Home Planet News	International Poetry Review
Maryland Poetry Review	Mid-American Review
the new renaissance	Northwest Review
Oxford Magazine	Poetry East
Puerto del Sol	Rohwedder
Snail's Pace Review	The Sun

Three of these poems appeared in the anthology, *The Age of Koestler* (Nicolaus Kogon, editor), Practices of the Wind Press, 1994.

I would like to thank Eugénio de Andrade for his patient assistance and kind hospitality. I would also like to thank Clara Pires, the ideal translator's consultant, for her good-humored help and friendship. In addition, I would like to acknowledge the support of the State University of New York at Plattsburgh.

Introduction

EUGÉNIO DE ANDRADE was born in 1923 in Povoa da Atalaia, a small village in rural Portugal not far from the Spanish border. He was raised by a much beloved mother, whose death in 1956 deeply affected him. His feelings for his father may be deduced from that figure's total absence in his writings.

Mother and son moved to Lisbon, and it was there, at the age of twelve, that Eugénio de Andrade first discovered poetry. He began spending much time in public libraries, reading and writing, and his first published poem, "Narcissus," appeared when he was sixteen. Three years later his first book, *Adolescence,* appeared. These early efforts, along with *Purity,* a second collection published in 1945, were later disowned by the poet as juvenilia. Of his early writings, he has preserved only ten poems in his *Complete Poetry and Prose.*

In 1948, *Hands and Fruit (As Mãos e os Frutos)* appeared to critical acclaim. Now in its fourteenth edition, it marked Eugénio de Andrade's indisputable arrival as a poet. Two years after its publication, he moved to Porto, the commercial center of the North, where he assumed a position in the

Department of Health and Social Welfare, remaining there till his retirement in 1983. Although residing quietly in Porto for forty-four years, the poet has regularly attended conferences and managed to travel a good deal, especially in Spain, Italy, France, and Greece. International poetry congresses and reading tours have taken him to Morocco, Macao, China, the Canaries, the Azores, and Mexico, as well. In 1988, he and I took a six-week reading tour of the United States and Canada, the first such extended tour by a Portuguese writer. Not only have these travels helped disseminate the poet's work, but many of the places visited have later reappeared in his poems.

After twenty-five years in the same modest, rather cramped apartment, overflowing with books and paintings, the poet this year moved to a four-story house where the Fundação Eugénio de Andrade has established a museum, a library, archives, and living quarters for him, his god-son Miguel, and Miguel's parents. Wide windows face the open Atlantic. Still settling in, the poet maintains he will travel no more.

Hands and Fruit has to date been followed by twenty-two more volumes of poetry, three collections of prose, two books for children, numerous anthologies, and translations into Portuguese of Sappho, Garcia Lorca, Yannis Ritsos, and the famous Portuguese letters, attributed to Sister Mariana Alcoforado, but known only from a French edition. There are nine recordings of Eugénio de Andrade's poems, three by the author himself. In addition, many of his poems have been set to music by Portugal's leading composers. There are even a dozen recordings of pop music with lyrics taken straight from his works.

Eugénio de Andrade's works have been translated into more than twenty foreign languages, including Spanish, French, Italian, Greek, Serbo-Croatian, Rumanian, Bulgarian, Hungarian, Czech, Russian, German, Dutch, Swedish, Norwegian, and English. A dozen volumes of his work have appeared in France and another dozen in Spain, where he has been translated not only into Spanish, but also into Bable (an Asturian dialect), Catalan, and Galego. In the United States, my translations of his work have appeared in close to one hundred literary magazines and in a handful of anthologies. They have also resulted in four books published prior to *Solar Matter: Inhabited Heart* (Perivale Press, 1985), *White on White* (QRL, 1987), *Memory of Another River* (New Rivers Press, 1988), and *Slopes of a Gaze* (Apalachee Press, 1992), which won the first Fernando Pessoa Translation Prize from Columbia University's Translation Center.

Eugénio de Andrade has been the recipient of numerous literary awards, including the "Prémio da Critica" from the International Association of Literary Critics in 1986, the "Prémio D. Dinis" in 1988, the "Grande Prémio de Poesia" of the Portuguese Writers' Association in 1989, and the French "Priz Jean Malrieu" in 1989. Marguerite Yourcenar refers to "the well-tempered clavier" of his poems; the Mexican poet Angel Flores calls his "a classic language, that is to say, an enduring language that becomes richer at every reading"; and the Spanish poet and critic Angel Crespo writes that "his voice was born to baptize the world." More than a dozen books dealing with his work have appeared in Portugal, and he has garnered considerable critical attention in Spain, Italy, France, and Brazil. It is probably safe to say that, with the exception of the great Fernando Pessoa, Eugénio de Andrade has been translated and studied more than any other Portuguese poet of this century.

Matéria Solar was first published in 1980 and has gone through four editions. In 1985, a translation into Bable was published in Spain. The following year, a highly successful French translation appeared. Over the last twelve years, all the poems in this book have appeared in various literary magazines in the United States.

The title of this collection is a key to all of Eugénio de Andrade's work, for in its bold simplicity it focuses directly on what, for him, is at the heart of the human condition: man's fate as a creature of flesh, of matter. Children of the sun, heirs to warmth, joy, desire, passion, our best task is to burn intensely bright as we inevitably burn away. The inescapable paradox of life, that we are dying even as we are most violently alive, like wood being consumed on a hearth of dancing flames, remains the crux of human experience illumined by these poems. Our inevitable extinction is implicit in the title's substantive: *Matéria* — Matter. The possibly transcendent joy, heat, glory of our existence are suggested by the modifier *Solar,* a word that reverberates with energy throughout Eugénio de Andrade's work, and above all in this particular book. When a critic referred to him as a "solar poet," Eugénio was especially pleased.

In an interview concerning his previous book, *Memory of Another River,* the poet speculated that perhaps the book's original purpose was "to give a name to desire." Throughout Eugénio de Andrade's work, desire seems to represent the highest human manifestation of man's solar nature. In the present volume, poem after poem reveals a close linkage between sun imagery and the life-affirming force of desire. As early as poem #5, the connection is made explicit: "isn't desire/ the closest friend of the sun?" In poem #7, after speaking of summer's fragrance and "frenzy of the cicadas," the poet shifts to a human body: "That's what blinds you, the sunlight of the flesh." The explicitly sexual poem #10, concluding with the lines, "A naked torso—/and the light quivers," is echoed by poem #20: "A naked body./And the seashore thrashed/by the sun and someone's gaze." A powerful love poem (#25) begins with the admonition, "Be still, light burns between the lips," and poem #37 refers to "the juice/or the sun of the mouth." Characteristically, in Eugénio de Andrade's poetry, the mouth, whether the instrument of language or of love, is always the focus of desire.

Another poem, here reproduced in full, deliberately confounds the mouth and sun:

But how to make it last
to the final moment,
this mouth, this sun?

One must love it,
lofty and patient,
where the flame chants.

Love it. Till the end,
Till it turns to dance.

Here we have not only a further example of mouth and sun as life-affirming images, but also the poet's attempt to deal with the dark corollary of our blazing life: the fact that it must end. His response to our human dilemma is simple and direct: to love what we have ("this mouth, this sun") while we have it — "Till it turns to dance." In this poem, the poet's enchantment with the sun does not prevent him from seeing the encroaching shadows of the night.

In fact, a good number of the later poems in this collection show a growing uneasiness, reflected in the title of his subsequent book, *The Weight of the Shadow (O Peso da Sombra,* 1982). Already in poem #13, he speaks of himself as the "sun's accessory" boldly and ominously immersed "in this blaze of body to the end." In #30, after plunging his fingers "deep into the sun," he ruefully reflects on "the body ever losing in the face of days," and in the next poem the passage of time is even clearer as he watches "walls crumble" and says "good-bye to the leaves." In a later poem he rhetorically asks: "What remains of autumn's amorous instruments?" A pessimistic answer is suggested by the image of a final season encroaching: "See how one slowly dies/in this winter/edging toward our waist." And in poem #45, images of winter rain and desert combine to suggest exhaustion and defeat:

> It's raining, this is the desert, the fire's gone out,
> what to do with these hands, the sun's accomplices?

This is followed by a cry of apparent desperation in #47, where the poet exclaims "This is what I am/a tortured branch of the sun." And in the next poem, with bitterness, he advises himself to "abandon this thin sun."

In the end, however, having confronted extinction, the poet seems to sense in his Solar Matter hints of eternity, and he rallies himself to declare "I say that I was here, and now I go/ the route of another, whiter sun." And it is this route that Eugénio de Andrade hopes his poems will illuminate for him, as they pass on to us and future readers their solar light.

Alexis Levitin
Lisbon
July, 1994

Preface to the English Edition

Whitman and the Squirrels

NOT LONG AGO, when I arrived at Pedras Rubras Airport after a short stay in America, a journalist asked me what I had liked most in the States.

"The squirrels," I answered, without a moment's hesitation.

"The squirrels? Didn't you like anything else?"

"Not as much as the squirrels, no."

The journalist must have not believed his ears, but I swear I was telling him the truth. More than the splendor of autumn in Vermont or of the Cloisters in New York, more than the redwoods of Muir Woods or the children's library in Menlo Park, more than the bison on the outskirts of Plattsburgh or the Whaling Museum of New Bedford — and these are things that I loved — it was those squirrels, which I had never seen before and which I came upon in all parts of

America, that fascinated me. I was so in love with those marvelous creatures that, at the universities through which I passed, I would throw out the idea (and I wonder if it managed to take root in some of the more subtle spirits) that the stars of the American flag ought to be replaced by squirrels. Many, many days have passed since then, yet the idea still seems to make sense to me — from Big Sur to Niagara Falls, from the cemetery at Camden to Monterey Bay, in any space, no matter how confined, wherever a few tufts of grass grew or there was a tree to climb, there they were — squirrels! They and Whitman and Melville are America — and all of them have entered my poems. I hope they feel at home, and may they survive there for many years.

America is not part of the mythology of my youth. The culture I took in was Mediterranean, with some touches from the Orient. *Leaves of Grass* and *Moby Dick* only reached me when I was already on my way to manhood. And it would be another five or six years before I would see an exhibition in Paris on Frank Lloyd Wright and his "Fallingwater." As we can see, they are just three, my Americans, but Whitman, Melville and Wright are worth a continent. To the first of these men it would fall to play a prominent role in my life. I say life, not poetry, for "Song of Myself," "Calamus," and "Children of Adam" were the solar shock waves that opened fissures in my soul; it was above all the image of the new man, that image of a "semi-divine vagabond that the verses revealed," as Borges put it, that helped me to be *"plus moi-même que moi.* " In Whitman, the poetry hesitated between the house of the soul and that of the spirit, and no one reading it could fail to feel himself his friend, his brother, or his lover.

Bit by bit, I began to grow closer to America; sometimes, however, I would also draw back. I read wonderful poems by Emily Dickinson, Eliot, Stevens, Williams, Marianne Moore; I also read some marked by a most provincial pedantry (Pound), or by an exhibitionism bordering on the sordid (Ginsberg). While in America, I saw the most beautiful architecture of our times and that painting of Hopper's, "Early Sunday Morning," for which I can find no adjectives. But I also saw the imbecile "artistic" experiments of Warhol promoted by a totally brainless media. I was moved by those black voices, illuminating the shadows with their spirituals. But I didn't find again the fraternal undulation from "the bottom of the sea of life" that the poetry of Whitman and Melville had brought me.

Perhaps these words will make sense at the threshold to a book that, thanks to the attentive and friendly hand of Alexis Levitin, is now beginning its American journey, under the solar sign of the squirrels and Walt Whitman.

Porto, July 1993
Eugénio de Andrade

Solar Matter
Matéria Solar

1

Podias ensinar à mão
outra arte,
essa de atravessar o vidro;

podias ensiná-la
a escavar a terra
em que sufocas sílaba a sílaba;

ou então a ser água,
onde, de tanto olhá-las,
as estrelas caíam.

1

You could teach the hand, perhaps,
another art, that of penetrating glass;
you could teach it how
to burrow down into the earth
on which you suffocate by syllables;

or else to turn to water,
into which the stars, from being
so much gazed at, fall.

2

O muro é branco
e bruscamente
sobre o branco do muro cai a noite.

Há um cavalo próximo do silêncio,
uma pedra fria sobre a boca,
pedra cega de sono.

Amar-te-ia se viesses agora
ou inclinasses
o teu rosto sobre o meu tão puro
e tão perdido,
ó vida.

2

The wall is white
and suddenly
night falls upon the whiteness of the wall.

There is a horse close to silence,
a cold stone on its mouth,
a stone blind for sleep.

I would love you if you now would come
or bend
your face over mine, so pure,
so lost,
oh life.

3

Havia
uma palavra
no escuro.
Minúscula. Ignorada.

Martelava no escuro.
Martelava
no chão da água.

Do fundo do tempo,
martelava.
Contra o muro.

Uma palavra.
No escuro.
Que me chamava.

3

There was
a word
in the dark.
Minuscule. Unremarked.

Hammering in the dark.
Hammering
at the water's heart.

From the bowels of time,
hammering.
At the wall.

A word.
In the dark.
For me. A call.

4

Este sol, não sei se já o disse,
este sol é o mar todo
da minha infância.

É como se fora manhã alta,
os seus cabelos ardem,
mas eu sonho com outra boca.

Onde aprenda a ser água.

4

This sun, have I already said this,
this sun was all my sea
in childhood.

As if it were late morning,
hair is on fire,

yet I dream of another mouth.
Where I may learn to turn to water.

5

Claro que os desejas, esses corpos
onde o tempo não enterrou ainda
os cornos fundo — não é o desejo
o amigo mais íntimo do sol?
Que os desejas, como se cada um
deles fosse o último, último corpo
que o teu corpo tivesse para amar.

5

Of course you want them, those bodies
where time has not yet buried
deep its horns — isn't desire
the closest friend of the sun?
Yes, you want them, as if each
one were the last, the last body
your body would ever have for loving.

6

A tarde sacudiu as suas crinas,
as crianças demoram-se nos espelhos,
um amigo começa no verão,
no íntimo despir das suas luzes.

6

The afternoon shakes its mane,
children linger in mirrors,
a friend begins in summer,
in the intimate unveiling of light.

7

Conhecias o verão pelo cheiro,
o silêncio antiquíssimo
do muro, o furor das cigarras,
inventavas a luz acidulada
a prumo, a sombra breve
onde o rapazito adormecera,
o brilho das espáduas.
É o que te cega, o sol da pele.

7

You knew summer by its fragrance,
the ancient silence
of the wall, the frenzy of the cicadas,
you invented the slightly bitter perpendicular
light, the brief shadow
in which a young urchin had dropped asleep,
the luster of his shoulder blades.
That's what blinds you, the sunlight of the flesh.

8

O sorriso.
O sorriso aberto
contra o muro.

Exactamente
como as ervas,
é muito antigo.

E sobre as ervas
e o muro
debruça-se no caminho.

Quem o arranca,
e levará consigo?

8

A smile.
An open smile
against the wall.

Just
like the grass,
it is old, very old.

And over the grass
and the wall
it leans toward the road.

Who will pluck it
and take it with him?

9

Outra vez o pátio vidrado da manhã.
Vais surgir e dizer : eu vi um barco.
Era quando aos lábios me chegava
a porosa argila de outros lábios.
Estava então a caminho de ser ave.

9

Once again the courtyard glazed with morning.
You will rise up and say: I saw a boat.
It was when there came to my lips
the porous clay of other lips.
Then I was on my way to becoming bird.

10

A manhã parada.
O azul.
A fundura da pupila.

Não é ainda a sede,
a matilha,
a febre.

O tronco nu —
a luz vacila.

10

Morning stopped still.
Blueness.
The pupil's depths.

It isn't thirst, as yet,
the hounds unleashed,
fever.

A naked torso —
and the light quivers.

11

É quando a chuva cai, é quando
olhado devagar que brilha o corpo.
Para dizê-lo a boca é muito pouco,
era preciso que também as mãos
vissem esse brilho, dele fizessem
não só a música, mas a casa.
Todas as palavras falam desse lume,
sabem à pele dessa luz molhada.

11

It is when the rain falls, it is when
looked at slowly, that the body glistens.
To tell of it the mouth is not enough,
one's hands, as well, would have to see
that glistening and make of it
not only music, but a dwelling place.
All words speak that flame,
the flavor of flesh from that moist light.

12

Tocar-te a pele,
o pulso aberto
ao gume do olhar.

Que seja esse
o chão, o sopro
do primeiro dia.

Rosa inflamável,
boca do ar.

12

To touch your skin,
pulse open
to a look's sharp edge.

Let this be
the earth, the breath
of the first day.

Combustible rose,
mouth of the air.

13

Aqui me tens, conivente com o sol
neste incêndio do corpo até ao fim:
as mãos tão ávidas no seu voo,
a boca que se esquece no teu peito
de envelhecer e sabe ainda recusar.

13

Here you have me, sun's accessory
in this body blazing to the end:
hands so eager in their flight,
mouth which on your breast forgets
to age, while knowing still how to refuse.

14

O sol,
a poeira
lentíssima do sul,

a pedra do ar
clara e mordida,

a branca e nua
e tão antiga
poeira do sol,

vem pousar-me
nos olhos.

Ainda.

14

The sun,
the slowest
southern dust,

the stone of air,
clear and bitten,

the white and naked
and most ancient
dust of the sun,

settling, settling
on my eyes.

Still.

15

O que respira em ti são os olhos,
o azul de um sol sem rugas,
as primeiras águas da carícia.

O sabor a barco que tem a boca! —
a isto se chama juventude, às vezes,
ou estrela de sangue vivo.

De costas para a noite, a terra
enquanto arde é quase um rio.

15

What breathes in you are your eyes,
the blue of an unfurrowed sun,
first waters of a caress.

How the mouth tastes of boat —
this is called youth, sometimes,
or star of living blood.

With back turned to night, the earth
while it burns is almost a river.

16

Tu estás onde o olhar começa
a doer, reconheço o preguiçoso
rumor de agosto, o carmim do mar.

Fala-me das cigarras, desse estilo
de areia, os pés descalços,
o grão do ar.

16

You are where my gaze begins
to ache, I recognize the lazy
murmur of August, the carmine of the sea.

Speak to me of cicadas, of that special
sand, your bare feet,
the grain of the air.

17

São fáceis de encontrar, os meus amigos,
vejo-os nesses lugares marítimos,
a tardia floração dos olhos,
o difícil comércio das palavras,
o corpo do verão sobre os joelhos.

17

I find my friends with ease;
I see them in those places by the sea,
the late blossoming of their eyes,
the difficult commerce of words,
summer's body across their knees.

18

Eu amei esses lugares
onde o sol
secretamente se deixava acariciar.

Onde passaram lábios,
onde as mãos correram inocentes,
o silêncio queima.

Amei como quem rompe a pedra,
ou se perde
na vagarosa floração do ar.

18

I loved those places
where the sun
in secret gave itself to be caressed.

Where lips have passed,
where hands have innocently run,
silence burns.

I loved like one who shatters rock
or loses self
in the languid flowering of the air.

19

A mão, a terra prometida
cada vez mais distante, só a mão
sabe ainda o caminho.

Um corpo não é casa da tristeza
e eu sempre pousei à entrada
da pedra do verão.

Ó pedra pedra - pedra de alegria.
Exasperada.

19

The hand, the promised land
always further off, only the hand
still knows the way.

A body is not a house of sorrow,
and I always settled on the threshold
of the stone of summer.

Oh stone, stone — stone of joyfulness.
Exasperated.

20

Tocar um corpo
e o ar
e a língua da neve.

Tocar a erva
mortal e verde
de cinco noites
e o mar.

Um corpo nu.
E as praias fustigadas
pelo sol e o olhar.

20

To touch a body
and air
and the snow's tongue.

To touch the grass
mortal and green
of five nights
and the sea.

A naked body.
And the seashore thrashed
by the sun and someone's gaze.

Agora são elas que têm o teu rosto,
as palavras; e não só o rosto:
o sexo e a trémula alegria
que foi sempre senti-lo desperto.
Sem palavras já não somos nada;
estão agora de perfil, repara
como reflectem o que de juvenil
houve sempre em ti, o mesmo sorriso
só um pouco menos fatigado
e o andar apenas menos lento.

21

Now it is they who have your face,
the words; and not your face alone:
your sex and the trembling joy,
always, at feeling it awake.
Without words we are nothing anymore;
now they are in profile, note
how they reflect something young
you always had in you, the same smile,
only a little less tired,
the same gait, only a little less slow.

22

Agrada-me estar aqui, falar
de árvores, dizer delas
o que disse da neve noutra ocasião.

Da janela avista-se a torre
sobre as águas, as da infância
ou da loucura, pois não há outras

assim tão inocentes, e tão próximas
do coração da terra — dizer delas
o que noutra ocasião disse da neve.

22

I am pleased to be here, to speak
of trees, to say of them
what I said of snow at another time.

From the window one can see the tower
over the waters, waters of childhood
or of madness, for there are no others

so very innocent and so close
to the earth's heart — to say of them
what at another time I said of snow.

23

Este país é um corpo exasperado,
a luz da névoa rente ao peito,
a febre alta à roda da cintura.

O país de que te falo é o meu,
não tenho outro onde acender o lume
ou colher contigo o roxo das manhãs.

Não tenho outro, nem isso importa,
este chega e sobra para repartir
com os corvos — somos amigos.

23

This country is an exasperated body,
a glimmer of fog close to its breast,
high fever circling its waist.

The country which I tell you of is mine,
there is no other where I can light a fire
or collect with you the amaranth of morning.

I have no other, nor does it matter,
this one's enough, and then some, for sharing
with the crows — they are my friends.

É o que desejas, que pela porta
estreita passe o ar, a extraviada
e impossível voz do amigo,

que passem os pés miúdos
e brancos da poeira,
a bica de água, a manhã de vidro.

24

That's what you want, that through the narrow
door air may enter, the lost and wandering
impossible voice of a friend,

that the diminutive white
steps of the dust might enter,
a flowing waterspout, a glassy morning.

Cala-te, a luz arde entre os lábios
e o amor não contempla, sempre
o amor procura, tacteia no escuro,
esta perna é tua?, é teu este braço?,
subo por ti de ramo em ramo,
respiro rente à tua boca,
abre-se a alma à língua, morreria
agora se mo pedisses, dorme,
nunca o amor foi fácil, nunca,
também a terra morre.

25

Be still, light burns between the lips
and love does not ponder, always
love searches, touches in the dark,
this leg, is it yours? is this your arm?
I climb you branch by branch,
breathe close to your mouth,
the soul opens itself to the tongue, I would die
now if you asked me to, sleep,
love was never easy, never,
the earth also dies.

Mas como fazer durar
até ao último instante
esta boca, este sol?

É preciso amá-la,
paciente e alta,
onde a chama canta.

Amá-la. Até ao fim.
Até ser dança.

26

But how to make it last
to the final moment,
this mouth, this sun?

One must love it,
lofty and patient,
where the flame chants.

Love it. Till the end.
Till it turns to dance.

27

Vacilantes perdem-se agora os dedos,
o mar é longe, vai-se a voz quebrando,
para morrer vai sendo tarde.

Não duvides: já fui essa árvore,
essa alegria só prometida às aves.

27

Hesitant, the fingers now are getting lost,
the sea far off, the voice now faltering;
for dying it is growing late.

Have no doubt; I was that tree,
that joyfulness promised only to birds.

28

Dormíamos nus
no interior dos frutos.

É o que temos: sono
e a estiagem subitamente
até ao fim.

Amargos.

Pela humidade descia-se
às fontes — lembro-me.
Dos lábios.

28

We were sleeping naked
deep within the fruit.

That's what we have: drowsiness
and a sudden drought
unto the end.

Bitter. Bitter.

Through moistness we descended
to the source — I remember.
Those lips.

29

Donde vêm?
De que rosto, de que estrela?

Apenas uma arde no vento.
As outras, fico a ouvi-las
escorrer da pedra.

Apenas uma em silêncio brilha.
As outras mordem
um coração de homem.

Só prometido à terra.

29

From where do they come?
From what face, from what star?

One alone burns in the wind.
As for the others, intent I listen
to them trickling from stone.

One alone in silence glistens.
The others bite
at a man's heart.

Promised to the earth alone.

30

Levei as mãos aos olhos para ver
se mesmo em ruína inda existias,
mergulhei no sol os dedos todos,
vêm molhados das águas fatigadas —
o corpo perdia-se frente aos dias.

30

I brought my hands up to my eyes to see
if even in ruins you still exist,
I plunged my fingers deep into the sun,
they come back wet with weary waters —
the body ever losing in the face of days.

31

Eu vi essas muralhas ruírem
sobre o rio — eram calmas as águas
de setembro, e sucessivas.

Despedia-me das folhas,
também eu preparava esse abandono
da cidade e das suas almas.

Eu vi essas muralhas.
Eram espessas broncas frias.
Ruíram, quando as olhava.

I saw those walls crumble
above the river — the September flow
was calm, and yet it went.

I said good-bye to the leaves,
and prepared as well for my desertion
of the city and its souls.

I saw those walls.
They were thick, rough, cold.
They crumbled as I watched.

32

Elas doíam-me, as estrelas,
como se tivera casa no ar.
Doíam-me, quando ao cair
ardiam às portas da água.
Como se eu fosse uma delas.

32

They hurt me, the stars,
as if my home were in the air.
They hurt me, as falling
they burned at the gateway to water.
As if I were what they are.

Moro agora nos olhos das crianças,
disponho a luz para as ver melhor,
o azul aproxima-se da pupila.
Nesta praça que me lembra outra
mais antiga, os pombos vêm
beber a solidão das minhas mãos.

Digamos então que um brusco aroma
me traz o sol ou uma abelha
ou esses olhos onde agora moro.

33

I dwell now in the eyes of children,
I move the light to see them better,
the blue comes closer to the pupil of my eye.

In this square reminding me of another
older one, the pigeons come
to drink solitude from my hands.

Let us say then that a sudden fragrance
brings me the sun or a honeybee
or those eyes where I now dwell.

34

Aqui oiço o trabalho do outono:
arte de abelha, a chama verde
e breve.

Seria o meu amor se não fosse
definitiva sede,
país sem nome.

Já mal o vejo, argila branca,
o riso fácil, a luz quebrada
em dentes de áqua.

34

Here I listen to the work of autumn:
the art of the bee, its green
brief flame.

It would be my love if it were not
ultimate thirst,
country without name.

Already I scarcely see it, white clay,
an easy laugh, light broken
on the water's teeth.

35

Não me espanta se vir aproximar-se
um braço do rio, ou outro, no escuro.

Coisas assim sucedem quando
nos sentamos num banco de jardim
e aves passaram a caminho do sul.

Escuto na noite a ver se descubro
um indício, um rumor
de febre que anuncie o cantar

desse que dizem ser arauto do sono.

It doesn't startle me if an arm of the river
or another comes toward me in the dark.

Things like that happen when
we are seated on a bench in the park
and birds have just passed, heading south.

I listen in the night to try to find
a sign, a murmur
of the fever that foretells the song

of one they say is herald to sleep.

36

Pela manhã de junho é que eu iria
pela última vez.

Iria sem saber onde a estrada leva.

E a sede.

36

Through a June morning, that's how I would go
the very last time.
I would go not knowing where the road leads.

Or thirst either.

37

Que resta dos amorosos instrumentos
do outono? Vi-te morder a tristeza,
era amarga, o ar tremia.

Onde o desejo não rebenta,
onde a chama se não medir com a chama,
como falar do sumo
ou do sol da boca e das laranjas?

Não chames pedra viva ao que nem
sequer pode com o peso do ar,
não dês o meu nome
ao último crepúsculo do olhar.

What remains of autumn's amorous
instruments? I saw you bite sorrow,
it was bitter, and the air trembled.

Where desire does not burst forth,
where flame does not match with flame,
how can one speak of the juice
or the sun of the mouth and of oranges?

Don't call one who cannot even stand
the weight of air a living stone,
nor give my name
to the last gray twilight of a glance.

38

Era como se o tivessem exposto nu
na esperança de que o sol o esfolasse
ou a chuva lavasse aquela mancha
vinda das trevas do ventre materno,
das entranhas de todas as mães
de sua mãe, secretamente, até explodir
e ser flor aberta no seu corpo.

38

It was as if they had exposed him naked
in hopes the sun would flay his skin
or the rain might wash away that stain
come from the shadows of the mother's womb,
from the bowels of all the mothers,
of his mother, secretly, until, exploding,
it turns into an open flower on his body.

Nesses lugares,
nesses lugares onde o ar
perde a mão,
os meus amigos começam a morrer.

Falar tornou-se insuportável.
Falar dessa luz queimada.
Deserta.

Que fazer desta boca,
do olhar,
tão perto outrora de ser música?

39

In those places,
in those places where the air
loses its grip,
my friends begin to die.

To talk becomes unbearable.
To talk about that scorched light.
Deserted.

What to do with this mouth,
this gaze,
once so near to being music?

40

Como dormir,
como dormir com a chuva
caindo sílaba
a sílaba sobre os olhos?

Nunca te quis assim,
nunca:
os dedos todos cegos.

Coroado de espuma —
assim devia ser
o corpo.
E o lume.

40

How can one sleep,
how can one sleep with the rain
falling syllable
by syllable upon one's eyes?

I never wished you thus,
never:
fingers totally blind.

Crowned with spume —
that's how the body
should be.
And the flame.

41

Fazer do olhar o gume certo,
atravessar a água corrompida,
no avesso da sombra soletrar
o rosto ardido de sede antiga.

41

To turn a gaze into a perfect blade,
to cross corrupted water,
and on the shadow's further side to fumble forth
a face burning with an ancient thirst.

42

Vê como se morre devagar
neste inverno
que se aproxima da cintura;

como a chuva entra pelo sono
e a sombra mais amarga
se vai juntando à terra nua;

ou a fria chama da cal
tarda.

42

See how one slowly dies
in this winter
edging toward our waist;

how the rain enters our dreams
and that most bitter shadow
mingles with the naked earth;

or how the lime's cold flame delays.

43

O corpo aprende devagar
a conhecer a terra.
Com as ervas.

A noite perdeu os seus navios,
o homem o seu rosto,
o sol a razão.

Com as ervas.
A conhecer a terra.
Rente ao chão.

43

Slowly, the body learns
to know the earth.
With the grass.

The night has lost its ships,
the man his face,
the sun its reason.

With the grass.
To know the earth.
Close, close to the ground.

44

Setembro: que lugar
para dormir — ou nessas folhas
ardendo pelo chão da tarde.

Como partir, deixar deserta
a casa errante
e diminuta do olhar?

A que nos resta.

44

September: what a good place
to sleep — perhaps on these leaves
burning on the afternoon ground.

How to go on, to abandon
the wandering, diminutive
house of our gaze.

All that remains to us.

45

Chove, é o deserto, o lume apagado,
que fazer destas mãos, cúmplices do sol?

45

It's raining, this is the desert, the fire's gone out
what to do with these hands, the sun's accomplices?

Olha, já nem sei de meus dedos
roídos de desejo, tocava-te a camisa,
desapertava um botão,
adivinhava-te o peito cor de trigo,
de pombo bravo, dizia eu,
o verão quase no fim,
o vento nos pinheiros, a chuva
pressentia-se nos flancos,
a noite, não tardaria a noite,
eu amava o amor, essa lepra.

46

Look, I don't even know about my fingers anymore,
gnawed with desire, I touched your shirt,
undid a button,
imagined your breast the color of wheat,
or of a wild dove, perhaps,
the summer almost at an end,
the wind in the pines, the rain
foreseen upon your loins,
the night, soon the night would come:
I was in love with love, that leprosy.

47

Afinal eram mais de quatro,
os rios,
que sonhava sobre a garganta.

Não sei se dormem ou esqueceram
que nome tinham —
nenhum acode.

Esse sou eu,
atormentado ramo de sol.

47

In the end they were more than four,
the rivers
that I dreamed upon my throat.

I don't know if they're sleeping or if they've forgotten
what name they had —
not one responds.
This is what I am,

a tortured branch of the sun.

48

Agora sai de cena à tua maneira,
abandona esse sol magro
às cabras e aos cardos.

Sem ruído, mas também sem hesitar,
desprende-te desse desejo
que vacila frouxo sobre a palha.

Precisas mudar de mão, ou de clima;
ou de pele;
ou simplesmente de latrina.

48

Now leave the stage in your own way,
abandon this thin sun
to goats and thistles.

Without a sound, but also without hesitance,
free yourself from that desire
that weakly vacillates in the hay.

You need a change of hand, or of climate;
or of skin;
or simply of latrines.

49

Sei onde o trigo ilumina a boca.
Invoco esta razão para me cobrir
com o mais frágil manto do ar.

O sono é assim, permite ao corpo
este abandono, ser no seio da terra
essa alegria só prometida à água.

Digo que estive aqui, e vou agora
a caminho doutro sol mais branco.

49

I know where wheat illuminates the mouth.
I invoke that thought to cover myself
with the most fragile mantle of air.

Sleep is like that, it allows the body
this abandon, to lie in the breast of the earth,
a joy promised only to water.

I say that I was here, and now I go
the route of another, whiter sun.

Que fizeste das palavras?
Que contas darás tu dessas vogais
de um azul tão apaziguado?

E das consoantes, que lhes dirás,
ardendo entre o fulgor
das laranjas e o sol dos cavalos?

Que lhes dirás, quando
te perguntarem pelas minúsculas
sementes que te confiaram?

50

What did you do with the words?
What account will you give of those vowels
of a blue so pacified?

And of the consonants, what will you tell them,
burning midst the splendor
of the oranges and the horses' sun?

What will you tell them, when
they ask you of the tiny
seeds confided to your trust?

Photograph by Robin J. Brown

About the Translator

ALEXIS LEVITIN IS THE WINNER of an NEA Translation Award, a Gulbenkian Foundation Fellowship, a New York State Council on the Arts Translation Award, the Fernando Pessoa Translation Award from Columbia University, a Wheatland Foundation Grant, and a Betty A. Coladay Award for his translations of the works of Eugénio de Andrade. His translatiuons of de Andrade's works have been published in four books and in more than sixty magazines.

He is a Professor of English at SUNY-Plattsburgh and lives in upstate New York.

Index of First Lines

Index of First Lines

Titles Available from QED Press

Poetry

A Mendocino Portfolio *by Cynthia Frank & Hannes Krebs*
Stark poetry and evocative black and white photography.
$17.95   88 pages (case)   10" x 8"   0-936609-12-5

Messages: New and Selected Poems *by Luke Breit*
Poetry highly praised by Ernesto Cardenal and Norman Mailer.
$8.95   136 pages (paper)   5.5" x 8.5"   0-936609-17-6

Art

Paris Connections: African American Artists in Paris
For this book, editors Asake Bomani and Belvie Rooks won a Before Columbus Foundation American Book Award. Bilingual (French/English), full-color reproductions, biographies, bibliography, index.
$30.00   128 pages (paper)   8.5" x 10"   0-936609-25-7

Paris Connections: African and Caribbean Artists in Paris
Editors Asake Bomani and Belvie Rooks present another collection of bilingual (French/English) essays on African and Caribbean artists in Paris. Full-color reproductions, biographies, index.
$14.95   64 pages (paper)   8.5" x 8.5"   0-936609-26-5

Creative Nonfiction

Iron House *by Jerome Washington*
Winner of the 1994 Western States Arts Federation Award for Creative Nonfiction, this much-praised book about the "con artists, sex addicts, psychotics and dreamers" who inhabit our prisons is both funny and searing.
$18.95   176 pages (case)   5.5" x 8.5"   0-936609-33-8

Fiction

The Long Reach *by Susan Davis*
A daring first novel about lovers re-united throughout time and encountering one another in difficult situations.

$12.95	208 pages (paper)	5.5" x 8.5"	0-936609-27-3

Tales From The Mountain *by Miguel Torga*
Ivana Carlsen translates this extraordinary collection of powerful short stories by Portugal's Nobel Prize nominee.

$12.99	160 pages (paper)	5.5" x 8.5"	0-936609-23-0
$21.99	160 pages (case)	5.5" x 8.5"	0-936609-24-9

Coz *by Mary Pjerrou*
A young midwife is thrust into an elemental, cosmic battle between a witch and a powerful patriarch.

$10.95	224 pages (paper)	5.5" x 8.5"	0-933216-70-X

The Man Who Owned the Hogs *by Leonard Dugger*
A savage, elegant, iconoclastic satire that attacks the foundations of religion while telling a gripping, ultimately tragic story.

$21.95	208 pages (case)	5.5" x 8.5"	1-879384-18-3

Psychology/Counseling

Listening with Different Ears: Counseling People Over 60 *by James Warnick*
A practical guide for therapists, social workers and ministers.

$19.50	224 pages (paper)	6" x 9"	0-936609-28-1
$24.95	224 pages (case)	6" x 9"	0-936609-31-1

The Collected Works of Lydia Sicher: An Adlerian Perspective
Adele K. Davidson edits this definitive work of one whose "contribution to Individual Psychology is enormous and brilliant."
— *Dr. Harold Mosak, Adler School of Professional Psychology*

$24.95	572 pages (paper)	6" x 9"	0-936609-22-2

Biography

Hyla Doc: Surgeon in China through War and Revolution, 1924-1949, *edited by Elsie Landstrom*
The memoirs of an American woman who treated victims of the Rape of Nanking in war-torn China.
$12.95   310 pages (paper)   6" x 9"   0-936609-19-2

Hyla Doc in Africa, 1950-1961, *edited by Elsie Landstrom*
Hyla Doc brings her unique blend of medical skill and compassion to the bush country of Liberia.
$10.50   104 pages (paper)   6" x 9"   0-936609-32-X

Business

Take This Job and Sell It! The Recruiter's Handbook, *by Richard Mackie*
Richard Mackie, guru to headhunters, describes, step-by-step, how to earn $100,000 a year at home by recruiting and placing professionals at mid-sized companies.
$24.95   176 pages (paper)   8.5" x 11"   0-936609-30-3

Available at your local bookstore or from

QED Press
155 Cypress Street, Fort Bragg, CA 95437
(800) 773-7782 or (707) 964-9520
Fax (707) 964-7531